GREAT MINDS
of Ancient Science and Math

THE GREAT PHILOSOPHER

PLATO AND HIS PURSUIT OF KNOWLEDGE

Titles in the *Great Minds of Ancient Science and Math* Series:

THE GREATEST MATHEMATICIAN:
ARCHIMEDES AND HIS EUREKA! MOMENT
ISBN-13: 978-0-7660-3408-2

THE GREAT THINKER:
ARISTOTLE AND THE FOUNDATIONS OF SCIENCE
ISBN-13: 978-0-7660-3121-0

THE FATHER OF THE ATOM:
DEMOCRITUS AND THE NATURE OF MATTER
ISBN-13: 978-0-7660-3410-5

MEASURING THE EARTH:
ERATOSTHENES AND HIS CELESTIAL GEOMETRY
ISBN-13: 978-0-7660-3120-3

THE FATHER OF GEOMETRY:
EUCLID AND HIS 3-D WORLD
ISBN-13: 978-0-7660-3409-9

THE FATHER OF ANATOMY:
GALEN AND HIS DISSECTIONS
ISBN-13: 978-0-7660-3880-1

THE GREATEST DOCTOR OF ANCIENT TIMES:
HIPPOCRATES AND HIS OATH
ISBN-13: 978-0-7660-3118-0

THE GREAT PHILOSOPHER:
PLATO AND HIS PURSUIT OF KNOWLEDGE
ISBN-13: 978-0-7660-3119-7

GREAT MINDS
of Ancient Science and Math

THE GREAT PHILOSOPHER

PLATO AND HIS PURSUIT OF KNOWLEDGE

Mary Gow

Enslow Publishers, Inc.
40 Industrial Road
Box 398
Berkeley Heights, NJ 07922
USA

http://www.enslow.com

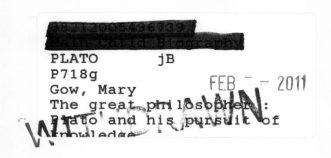
Copyright © 2011 by Mary Gow

Library of Congress Cataloging-in-Publication Data

Gow, Mary.
    The great philosopher : Plato and his pursuit of knowledge / Mary Gow.
      p. cm. — (Great minds of ancient science and math)
    Includes bibliographical references and index.
    ISBN 978-0-7660-3119-7
    1. Plato—Juvenile literature. I. Title.
  B395.G47 2011
  184—dc22
  [B]
                      2009044566

Printed in the United States of America

052010 Lake Book Manufacturing, Inc., Melrose Park, IL

10 9 8 7 6 5 4 3 2 1

To Our Readers: We have done our best to make sure all Internet Addresses in this book were active and appropriate when we went to press. However, the author and the publisher have no control over and assume no liability for the material available on those Internet sites or on other Web sites they may link to. Any comments or suggestions can be sent by e-mail to comments@enslow.com or to the address on the back cover.

Every effort has been made to locate all copyright holders of material used in this book. If any errors or omissions have occurred, corrections will be made in future editions of this book.

♻ Enslow Publishers, Inc., is committed to printing our books on recycled paper. The paper in every book contains 10% to 30% post-consumer waste (PCW). The cover board on the outside of each book contains 100% PCW. Our goal is to do our part to help young people and the environment too!

Illustration Credits: Corbis, p. 16; Courtesy of History of Science Collections, University of Oklahoma Libraries, pp. 12, 87, 104; Elizabeth Hewitt, pp. 29, 30, 32, 46, 54, 60; Enslow Publishers, Inc., p. 22; Getty Images/clipart.com, pp. 42, 56–57; Getty Images/photos.com, p. 3; Jeannie Sargent, pp. 76, 94, 96, 107 ; Ludovisi Collection, p. 101; © Marie-Lan Nguyen/Wikimedia Commons, pp. 40–41; Mary Gow, p. 73; National Aeronautics and Space Administration (NASA), p. 97; Wikimedia Commons, pp. 49, 64–65.

Cover Illustration: Getty Images/photos.com.

CONTENTS

"A Good Talk"

IN THE OPENING LINES OF PLATO'S *Republic,* the character Socrates describes a chance meeting with friends. He had been at Piraeus, the harbor complex for Athens. The great wooden ships of Athens' navy were anchored there. The port bustled with activity. Socrates and his friend Glaucon had been at a religious festival.

> I went down yesterday to the Piraeus with Glaucon, the son of Ariston, to pay my devotions to the goddess, and also because I wished to see how they would conduct the festival. . . .
>
> I thought the procession of the citizens very fine, but it was no better than the show made by the marching of the Thracian contingent.
>
> After we had said our prayers and seen the spectacle we were starting for town when Polemarchus . . . caught sight of us from a distance as we were hastening

homeward and ordered his boy run and bid us to wait
for him.[1]

Socrates and Glaucon paused, letting
Polemarchus catch up to them. Polemarchus
hoped that Socrates would stay. A torchlight
horse race planned for that evening promised
to be exciting. Polemarchus suggested they dine
together, and "go out and see the sights and meet
a lot of the lads there and have a good talk."[2]

In the *Republic*—a series of fictional
conversations written almost twenty-four hundred
years ago—Socrates did stay and talk. With
Glaucon, Polemarchus, and other "lads," Socrates
explored ideas of justice, truth, and goodness. In
far-reaching discussions, they talked about the
ideal state and how to train men to become wise
rulers. Prodded by Socrates' questioning, they
examined differences between the material world
we perceive with our senses and abstract ideas we
grasp with our minds. Logical and thoughtful,
the *Republic* still inspires readers to join the
conversation—to think critically and deeply about
important issues.

Plato, author of the *Republic,* is one of the most famous philosophers of all time. Philosophy today is defined as the rational investigation of questions about existence, knowledge, and ethics. Ethics deals with ideas of right and wrong behavior. To the Greeks, philosophy was the term for serious intellectual pursuits.[3] The Greek word *philos* means "love"; *sophia* is "wisdom." Philosophy was the love of wisdom. In Plato's time, philosophy included many subjects.

Plato's Philosophy of Science

Born around 428 B.C., Plato was the son of a wealthy and politically connected Athenian family. A well-educated young man, he was profoundly influenced by Socrates, a philosopher who explored morality and ethical conduct. As portrayed by Plato, Socrates lived for philosophy and died for it. Socrates was convicted by an Athenian jury and executed because of his influence on the young and his religious beliefs. Plato, with his connections, education, and wealth, might have chosen a life of public leadership in

Athens. Instead he followed Socrates' example and dedicated himself to philosophy. Plato lived to be eighty-one, leaving a legacy of thought that still influences us today.

Besides inquiring into philosophical subjects, Plato wrote and taught about them. Amazingly, all of his known written works still exist. More than twenty-five Platonic texts have been passed down through the centuries. Almost all of his texts are dialogues—fictional conversations. Plato himself is only briefly mentioned in a couple of them. His former teacher, Socrates, is the main figure in most.

Plato explored an astounding range of topics. In his writing he investigated political theory, virtue, language, art, love, mathematics, and religion.[4] The human soul and design of the universe were among his interests. Plato is even the source of the myth of the lost city of Atlantis. Few of Plato's dialogues focus on subjects that we now consider science. However, he made significant contributions to the long process that built modern science.

One subject that philosophers investigate is knowledge. "What is knowledge?" and "How do we know what we know?" are philosophical questions. Plato did not accept assumptions or opinions as knowledge. In the conversations of Plato's dialogues he exposes contradictions and false assumptions. With thoughtful questions, he opens inquiries into underlying truth.

To further the pursuit of knowledge, Plato founded the Academy, a center of learning. Although its teachings changed over the years, the school nurtured generations of thinkers. The philosopher Aristotle studied at the Academy for twenty years. He became one of its senior associates during Plato's lifetime. Biology, physics, zoology, and astronomy are among the dozens of subjects advanced by Aristotle. He established the way science would be practiced for two thousand years. Eratosthenes, a Greek thinker who measured the circumference of Earth, also studied there. Many other noted mathematicians and philosophers spent time at the Academy.

Plato did not make any specific scientific

In Italian artist Raphael's 1509 painting, *School of Athens*, Plato (left) walks beside his student Aristotle (right). Plato points upward, symbolizing his belief that true knowledge is found in abstract thought. Aristotle gestures downward, symbolizing his belief that the physical world is more worthy of study.

discoveries. His contribution was his "philosophy of science."[5] Plato did not look to physical things to find truth; he turned to reason and thought. He believed that abstract ideas held the answers to fundamental questions about the universe and humanity. Plato suggested that abstract entities, sometimes called Forms, were real objects of knowledge. Plato asserted that reason, rather than perception by our senses, leads to knowledge.[6] Material things we can see or touch are always changing—they are in flux. Living things change; animals, including people, are born, mature, and die. Inanimate things change, too; a volcano erupts, wood burns to ash, water evaporates. In Plato's view, changeable, physical things could not be true objects of knowledge. Objects of knowledge, he asserted, should always be known to be true. Numbers, for example, were objects that Plato recognized as unchanging.

Another of Plato's contributions to science was his cosmology—his explanation of the world and universe. Plato described an Earth-centered spherical universe, designed with order. In Plato's model, the sun, moon, and planets traveled around Earth in circular paths. The stars moved together as if set on a heavenly sphere. This was the accepted description of the cosmos for almost two thousand years. Even though Plato was incorrect about Earth's position in this system, his cosmology connects to our modern ideas. Plato believed that the universe had order and mathematical structure.[7]

It was a long journey from Plato to modern science. Today, we understand that statements of mathematics can describe and predict many natural phenomena. We know that planets, including Earth, follow elliptical paths as they orbit the sun. Gravity, the force that keeps Earth in its orbit and people on its surface, is described mathematically. Astrophysicists today look to mathematics to find the edges of the expanding universe, to probe black holes, to study forming galaxies, and to solve other cosmic puzzles. Nuclear physicists use mathematics to explain the energy released by splitting atoms and subatomic particles. Like Plato, modern scientists use ideas that are abstract and unchanging, along with the resources of mathematics, to seek answers about the matter and motion of our universe.

Early Greek Science

The roots of modern science stretch back to the ancient Greeks. Science is the study and explanation of natural phenomena in an orderly way. Science is not the natural world—it is the system of knowledge that explains it. Plato and others nurtured its early development with their unprecedented ideas.

Beginning about 150 years before Plato, some ancient Greeks started looking at the natural world in a new way. Their approach was different from earlier views in two significant ways. First, these thinkers began looking for explanations of natural phenomena—explanations that did not rely on supernatural influences, like gods with magical powers. Second, they tried to find rational proof of their explanations. They discussed and scrutinized explanations, testing them to try to find real causes of natural events.[8]

This Roman mosaic from a home in Pompeii shows Plato in conversation with associates at the Academy.

We can see the Greeks' shift in perspective through a familiar event. Every day the sun rises in the east and sets in the west. It rises and sets farther north along the horizon in the northern hemisphere's summer, and farther south in the winter. Year after year, it follows the same pattern, every day rising and setting. The Greeks' rich mythology offered an explanation for the sun's apparent movement. According to their supernatural explanation, a team of mighty horses pulled the chariot of Helios, the sun-god, across the sky. This explanation left room for the horses and Helios to leave when they wished and follow the course they chose. However, from experience,

Greeks saw that the sun followed a recognizable pattern. With supernatural causes, phenomena like the sun's movement were individual and random. Some Greek thinkers were not satisfied with those explanations. They wanted to understand the order they observed in the world.

Thales, one early thinker, lived in the first half of the sixth century B.C. Thales thought that there must be one original substance that was the basis of all things. He suggested that this substance was water. Thales proposed that "the earth is held up by water and rides like a ship and when it is said to 'quake' it is then rocking because of the movement of the water."[9] Instead of crediting the god Poseidon, the "Earth-shaker," with these events, Thales was seeking a cause in nature.

Anaximander, a contemporary of Thales, proposed a model to explain the observed movements of the sun, moon, and stars. Earth was shaped like a cylinder with the inhabited lands on the top, suggested Anaximander. The heavenly bodies were in three rings of fire moving around this flat-topped cylinder. Anaximander also proposed a theory of the origins of animals including man. In myths, men were made by the gods. In Anaximander's view, animals were created from the "wet," and man was originally born to a kind of fish.[10]

Other Greek thinkers proposed their views of Earth and the heavens, and explanations for change. There was openness in their inquiries. Thinkers knew of each other's ideas and criticized and discussed them. Some theories could not stand up to much scrutiny and were rejected. Others were developed in greater detail by subsequent thinkers.

Empedocles was born around 493 B.C. He died in 433 B.C., shortly before Plato was born. Empedocles suggested that there were four original and simple elements. These were fire, air, earth, and water. These substances were not the same as the more than one hundred chemical elements recognized today. Empedocles theorized that all substances of the world were made of the four elements, mixed and remixed to have different properties. The four elements of Empedocles' philosophy endured in later science and medicine.

Thales, Anaximander, and Empedocles were philosophers. Their inquiries were rational investigations about existence. They are known as pre-Socratic philosophers, because they came before Socrates. Unlike the pre-Socratics, Socrates was interested in human behavior and how to live a good life.

Plato's philosophy included both kinds of inquiries. Like Socrates, he investigated ideas of moral behavior and ideas of virtue and goodness. Like the pre-Socratics, he wanted to understand the order of the cosmos.[11] Plato's way of discovering this order was to use reasoning—to question thoughtfully and seek rational answers.

Plato leads us to examine what we think we know. In his elegant style, he guides us to explore ideas alongside cultured and charming Greek men of his day. In the *Republic,* Socrates never did see the torchlight race. Instead, he and the "lads" talked about potters and doctors, shadows and sunlight, geometry, war, dogs, horses, and much more. Their conversation poses fundamental questions about how to live our lives, the public good, and the nature of knowledge. It is still thought-provoking and meaningful today.

SON OF ATHENS

"PLATO WAS THE SON OF ARISTON AND Perictione [or Petone] and a citizen of Athens; and his mother traced her family back to Solon," wrote Diogenes Laertius in his biographical entry on Plato in *The Lives and Opinions of Eminent Philosophers*. Diogenes Laertius lived in the third century A.D. and wrote about many notable ancient Greeks. Separated from Plato by about seven centuries, he drew on earlier biographies and accounts. Plato was famous in the ancient world and much was written about him. To complicate matters, ancient Greeks often composed fictional accounts about well-known people. Diogenes Laertius did not necessarily have reliable information about Plato.

Aristotle, who studied with Plato and likely knew him well, wrote about his teacher. Aristotle's comments are about Plato's ideas, rather than his life. Plato's own writings are intellectual, not autobiographical. He only briefly mentions himself in them. His dialogues show the lifestyle and manners of aristocratic men of his time, but they offer few personal glimpses.

Certain facts about Plato's life are widely accepted. He was born around 428 B.C. His mother and probably his father were Athenian

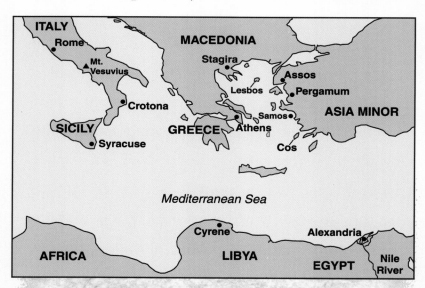

A map of Greece and the surrounding areas in Plato's time.

aristocrats. Aristocrats were members of wealthy, landowning families who traced their ancestry back to Athenian nobility before democracy.[2] Perictione, Plato's mother, was related to Solon, a great sixth century B.C. Athenian politician and poet. Laws written by Solon were building blocks of Athens' democracy. One of Perictione's cousins, Critias, was an influential politician in Plato's time. Plato's father died when Plato's mother was still quite young. She remarried and her new husband, Plato's stepfather, was also involved in Athenian government.

Plato was reportedly the youngest of four children. His brothers, Adiemantus and Glaucon, were several years older. Both brothers appear as intelligent and thoughtful characters in the *Republic*. Plato had one sister, Potone. Her son, Speusippus, studied with Plato and became director of the Academy after his uncle's death.

With his distinguished and wealthy family, Plato likely enjoyed a privileged childhood. According to Diogenes Laertius, he went to a well-known school. Private schools for boys were well established by Plato's time. There were no free or public schools then. Schooling generally started when a boy was around seven years old. Boys learned to read and write, studied music, and learned some basic arithmetic. They studied poetry, including Homer's epic poems the *Iliad* and the *Odyssey*. A family slave called a *paidagogos* accompanied a well-off boy like Plato to school.[3] Athletics were important in Greek education. Greeks were serious about sports and held competitions including the Olympic Games to honor the gods. These events included contests in running, throwing the javelin and discus, chariot races, and wrestling.

Wrestling was Plato's sport. The boy's wrestling coach supposedly gave him the nickname that identifies the philosopher to this day. According to Diogenes Laertius, Plato's birth name was Aristocles; he was named after his grandfather. The coach, Ariston of Argos, instead called the boy "Plato," which in Greek means "broad." Diogenes Laertius explained that there were three accounts for the nickname. Possibly, it was because of the boy's "robust figure." A second explanation was that his forehead was very wide. The most flattering suggestion was that it was because of the breadth of his eloquence.[4] Surprisingly, Diogenes Laertius commented that Plato had a very weak voice.[5]

Greece in Plato's time was not a unified country with a definable territory and a single government. The Greeks had dozens—even hundreds—of individual self-governing communities. This type of city-state was called a polis. Athens, Sparta, and Megara were among the polises located in the region of modern Greece. Others were dotted around the Mediterranean, some as far away as France, Spain, and Libya.

At its heart, a polis had a principal city or large town. Surrounding countryside, including farmland, forests, and nearby villages, was included in the polis. Mountain ranges, coastlines, or other natural boundaries often defined the territory of a polis. Each polis set its own laws. Each polis also defined its citizens' rights, like the right to a trial if accused of a crime. The polis determined its citizens' duties, like obligations to serve in the military. Some polises were ruled by tyrants or kings, others by groups of wealthy landowners. After Athens developed the first democracy, some other polises adopted that form of government.

Athens

Athens, Plato's home, was the largest Greek polis. Its population may have reached three hundred thousand people.[6] The polis's territory, known as Attica, was a triangular piece of land comprising some one thousand square miles. Separated from the north by mountains, Attica had a long coastline with fine harbors. Greeks were seafaring people, and Athens became a center of trade. The polis also developed a strong navy. Silver was among Attica's natural resources. The polis's mines were sources of wealth.

Athens in the fifth century B.C. was a magnificent city and a cultural and commercial hub. The Acropolis, a massive rock outcrop, stood at the heart of the city. The Acropolis was home to the sanctuary of the goddess Athena, daughter of Zeus. Athena was the goddess of just wars, but also the patroness of crafts like weaving, among other things. According to myths she emerged, fully grown and armed for battle, from her father's head.

Athena was a protectress of many cities, but had a special bond with the polis that bore her name. According to a famous myth, Athena and Poseidon, the god of the sea, competed for the Acropolis. Striking the ground on the hill with his trident, Poseidon produced a saltwater spring. Athena grew an olive tree. Olives were an important part of the Greek diet—eaten as fruit and also pressed for olive oil. Athena's gift was judged to be better and the Acropolis became her sanctuary.

In the fifth century B.C., Athens prospered, resulting in a massive public building spree and the construction of spectacular temples for the gods. Ruins of this grandeur still stand. At the time of Plato's birth, these impressive structures were new.

If we could see a photograph of Athens in

428 B.C., the year Plato was born, we would recognize some buildings. The Parthenon, with massive columns and finely executed relief sculptures, was completed in 432 B.C. Temples were not like modern churches where people go to religious services. Instead, they were earthly homes for the gods. A magnificent thirty-nine-foot-tall statue of Athena adorned with gold and ivory stood in the Parthenon. Her statue was carved by Phidias, one of the most famous Greek sculptors. An impressive entranceway to the Acropolis called the Propylaea had also just been finished.

The agora, Athens' downtown, was located just northwest of the Acropolis. This large open-air square was the center of polis life. Government buildings and temples surrounded it. Stoas, long buildings with columned porches, housed offices. A circular building, the Tholos, was a public dining hall and meeting room for officials. The council house and the mint, where Athenian silver coins were made, were in the agora. Several sanctuaries for the gods were there. With its shops and stalls,

The agora was the center of Athenian community life. The Hephaisteion, the temple in the background, was new in Plato's time. The low walls in the foreground are remains of the council house and other government buildings of his era.

the agora was the place for doing business with traders from other polises, for buying perfumes, pottery and grain, getting a haircut, hearing the news, and socializing.

A main road called the Panathenaic Way ran through the agora. Every summer a festival dedicated to Athena was celebrated in Athens.

The Greek word *pan* translates as "all" in English; this celebration was for all Athenians. In a huge procession, Athenians walked or rode horses or chariots along this road to the Parthenon. Every fourth year the celebration was especially grand with several days of music and athletic competitions. In this procession a glorious embroidered robe was ceremonially delivered to Athena's statue. The Panathenaic procession is depicted on the sculptured frieze of the Parthenon. A huge community feast of meat

Many Athenian government buildings were located in the agora. This circular foundation belonged to the Tholos, where officials held meetings and dined.

from sacrificed cattle and other animals was a highlight of this event.

Democracy

Certain functions of Athenian government took place in the agora. Some court sessions were held there. Committees that set agendas and handled parts of Athens' business met in the agora. The main site of Athens' citizen government in Plato's time, though, was on a nearby hillside called the Pnyx.

Beginning in the late sixth century B.C., several decades before Plato, Athenians began shaping a new type of government. This new political system of citizen rule is called democracy. The Greek word *demos* means "people"; *kratos* means "rule." *Democracy* means "the rule of the people." Under Athenian democracy, citizens had the right to vote and to make decisions for their community.

Athenian citizens met in the Assembly, a public meeting held about forty times a year. All citizens had the right to speak to the Assembly, arguing for or against decisions. They also had rights and responsibilities to hold public offices. Citizens had responsibilities to serve as jurors in Athenian courts—to hear trials and make decisions of guilt or innocence. Meetings of the Assembly were held outdoors on the hillside of the Pnyx. Citizens sat on benches facing a speaker's

The Athenian Assembly met on this hillside near the Acropolis. Citizens gathered in the open field that slopes to the left. Speakers stood on the bema, the stone platform jutting out from the wall, to address the Assembly.

platform. Six thousand citizens in attendance were required for a quorum, the minimum number needed to officially take action. The Assembly made decisions about foreign policy, they passed decrees. The Boule, a council of five hundred citizens, set the agenda for the Assembly, among other things.

In this remarkable system founded by the Athenians we see the importance of certain freedoms. Athenian citizens had equal opportunity to participate in government and they were entitled to equal treatment in court. Some citizens were wealthy, but most were not. Athenian aristocrats were citizens, but so were farmers, potters, and men who rowed the polis's warships. However, only about 10 percent of Athens' population were citizens.[7] Women, children, slaves, and foreigners were not citizens.

Greek women were not part of the polis's political life. Women's sphere of life and influence was in the home. Women are frequently seen in Greek art playing the lyre, sewing, weaving, or in ceremonies. In some religious ceremonies women had prominent roles. In myths, goddesses showed great spirit and often took on their male counterparts—as Athena did in winning the Acropolis. Mortal women, though, were not members of the Assembly and did not vote. In Athenian courts they had few rights.

Slavery was not only widely practiced in ancient Greece, it was part of the Greek economy. In battles, the victors typically took the people they defeated as slaves. Greeks called people who did not speak the Greek language "barbarians." There was apparently a widely held view that barbarians were suited to slavery.[8] Slaves had no rights and were viewed as possessions. Some Greek families had household slaves; some landowners had agricultural slaves who farmed their lands. Polises, including Athens, had publicly owned slaves who served as police and clerks or worked in the silver mines. During Plato's time, the slave population of Athens is estimated to have been eighty thousand to one hundred thousand— roughly a third of the population.[9]

As a son of Athens, Plato grew up seeing his

city's government in action. He also grew up in a time of war. Athens was a naval power. Sparta, a polis in the Peloponnesian peninsula, had a strong and disciplined army. The two states were at war from 431 B.C. to 404 B.C. Young Athenian citizens had duties to serve in the military, so Plato may have fought in some of these battles.

Sophists and Socrates

ARISTOCRATIC BOYS LIKE PLATO WENT TO schools from about age seven to their late teens. No colleges or universities existed then. Young men going into certain careers, like medicine, learned through apprentice-type arrangements. In the mid-fifth century B.C., a new educational option emerged.

Athens, with its democracy, valued public life. In the Assembly, a citizen who spoke well and convinced others to vote for his proposals was more likely to be successful than one who did not speak out. Effective public speakers might guide Athens' policies and actions. In the courts, a good speaker might convince a jury of an accused person's guilt or innocence. Many Athenian families wanted their sons to have the skills to be leaders.

Sophists

Sophist, like the word *philosophy,* has its root in *sophia,* the Greek word for "wisdom." Directly translated, a Sophist was a wise man. Sophists were self-proclaimed teachers. These were not members of a group who shared the same ideas. Sophists were individual teachers with considerable differences in their views and teaching. A broad range of subjects were taught by Sophists. Many were interested in natural philosophy. Some taught theories about the natural world, mathematics, geography, or history. Rhetoric was a popular subject. Rhetoric is the art of using language to persuade. Especially, though, Sophists taught *aretē,* which means "excellence" or "virtue." Morality and justice were issues that often arose in politics.[1] Convincingly arguing that a position was just or morally right could win debates.

There were no requirements to be a Sophist—

only a willingness to teach and an ability to draw clients who would pay for the instruction. Sophists were often travelling teachers. They charged money for their instruction and gave lectures in public. Athens' agora was a popular venue for their lectures.

Today we still know the names of many Sophists. A few, including Gorgias and Protagoras, appear in Plato's dialogues. Plato did not have a high regard for the Sophists. He did not consider them serious thinkers. He felt that they put on displays and did not seek truth.[2] Even with the Sophists' shortcomings, there was demand for these teachers, especially in Athens.

The Sophists are identified with the period from 450 B.C. to 380 B.C. Although there were Sophist writings, they have not survived. We know some of their teachings from quotes and references in the writings of other Greek authors. The Sophists are not credited with any specific contributions to scientific thought, but they belong to the rich cultural background that produced Plato and other thinkers.

Socrates

Socrates belonged to the same generation as the Sophists. He was born in the polis of Athens, but not in the main city, around 469 B.C. Socrates was the son of Sophroniscus and Phaenarete. Plato portrayed Socrates as a poor man who was not interested in material things. Socrates' family must have had some wealth, though, because he served as a hoplite in Athens' military.[3] Hoplites were warriors who marched into battle shoulder to shoulder, armed with spears and short swords.

The hoplites wore distinctive bronze helmets and armor and carried bronze shields. As the government did not pay for hoplites' weapons, these warriors had to have enough money to buy the expensive equipment themselves. Socrates reportedly fought courageously in three battles.[4]

A philosopher, intellectual, and citizen of Athens, Socrates greatly influenced Plato and other young Athenians. Socrates' main interest was moral virtue—how one should live life.[5] In Plato's writing, Socrates denies that he is a

This fragment of an ancient Greek vase depicts hoplite soldiers at war.

teacher. His questioning approach was different from the teaching style of the Sophists. Unlike them, he did not charge fees.

We do not know when Socrates started his philosophical pursuits. By 423 B.C., when Plato was about five years old, Socrates was famous enough

to be mocked in a popular satirical play. The playwright Aristophanes knew of Socrates. In his comedy *The Clouds,* Aristophanes showed a farcical Socrates teaching at a "Thinkery." There, students learned to make weak arguments appear strong. In the play, clouds were supposedly new gods that Socrates and his followers worshipped instead of Zeus and traditional Greek deities.[6]

While Sophists claimed to have knowledge of the topics they taught—to be authorities—Socrates took the opposite view. "I am only too conscious that I have no claim to wisdom great or small," he says in Plato's dialogue, the *Apology.*[7] Like the Sophists, Socrates was concerned with *aretē* or virtue. The path to virtue, he believed was not learned through lectures but through self-examination. True knowledge, Socrates believed, was of real and eternal things.

This illustration shows Socrates, dressed in a ragged white toga, discussing his ideas with men in the agora. His goal was to obtain knowledge, not wealth, so he did not charge fees for his lectures, unlike the Sophists.

Unlike the Sophists, Socrates taught by conversing directly with people. With thoughtful questions he guided them to examine their blindly held ideas. In an organized way, he asked them if they really knew what they were talking about. By the end of a conversation with Socrates, a man usually recognized that his views on a subject were inconsistent. Socrates' technique of systematic cross-examination is still used today. It is known as the Socratic Method.

Socrates' ideas were also different from those of earlier Greek philosophers. Thinkers including Empedocles and Thales tried to understand the world and its substances. Socrates' interest was man. Socrates "first called philosophy down from heaven, set her into the cities, introduced her into men's homes, and compelled her to investigate life and customs, good and evil," wrote Cicero, a Roman philosopher and statesman.[8] In other words, Socrates turned philosophy to human affairs. By introducing "her into men's homes," Cicero was saying Socrates showed that philosophy relates to everyone on a personal level.

Plato apparently began meeting with Socrates around 408 B.C. Plato at the time was about twenty years old, Socrates was around sixty years old. Plato was soon in the philosopher's inner circle. Socrates was influential with young Athenian aristocrats. Plato's uncle Critias, his brothers, and some friends who appear in his dialogues were also followers of Socrates.

Athenian democracy was a remarkable achievement. In Plato's time, it was also a hotly debated form of government.[9] Athenian democracy gave citizens, rich and poor, equal rights to speak to the Assembly, to vote, and to appear in the courts. Critics of democracy, especially wealthy property owners, did not necessarily agree that political decisions should be made by ordinary, even poor, men.[10]

During the Peloponnesian War from 431 B.C. to 404 B.C., there was sometimes strong anti-democratic feeling in Athens, especially when Athens was defeated by Sparta in battles. Athens surrendered to Sparta in 404 B.C. The Spartan general, Lysander, installed thirty Athenian citizens to run the government. These men became known as the Thirty Tyrants. They abolished Athens' jury system. The Thirty Tyrants executed hundreds of their opponents. Critias, Plato's uncle, was the leader of the Thirty Tyrants. The reign of the Thirty Tyrants did not last long. A band of pro-democracy Athenians defeated the Tyrants' army in 403 B.C. Critias was killed in the battle.[11]

Socrates was not prominent in Athens' government, but he did perform his duties of citizenship. He served on the Prytaneis, a council of the Boule. During his service, he was the only council member to oppose a vote which he believed was illegal. Later, he refused a government order to arrest a man he believed to be innocent.

In 399 B.C., after the Thirty Tyrants had been forced out of office and democracy was restored, Socrates was charged with two crimes. "Socrates is guilty of corrupting the minds of the young and of believing in deities of his own invention instead of the gods recognized by the state," was the accusation.[12] Socrates was tried in court. The case was heard by a jury of 501 Athenians. By a narrow margin, he was found guilty. For his crime, the Athenians sentenced him to death. Socrates' friendship with men who were critical

According to popular tradition, these cave rooms cut from the bedrock near the Athenian agora are known as "Socrates' Prison."

of democracy, his considerable influence, and his questioning approach were probably factors in his case.

Plato had high regard for Socrates. Plato believed that Socrates was the model of the true philosopher; living and dying for truth and knowledge.[13] Several of Plato's early writings are set in the last days of Socrates' life. The *Apology* is Plato's version of Socrates' defense to the jury. This speech is still thought-provoking.

After being found guilty and sentenced to death, Socrates was sent to prison, but he was not immediately executed. Among the Athenians' many traditions, each year they sent a ship carrying gifts to Apollo's sanctuary on the island of Delos. No executions were conducted in Athens from the day the ship left the city until it returned. Socrates spent almost a month in prison. There he continued meeting with his followers and exploring ideas. When the ship returned to Athens, Socrates was prepared for his death. His followers, though, were devastated that his end was so near. Plato himself was not with Socrates, at least as he reports it, but heard accounts from friends. In Plato's dialogue the *Phaedo*, a character gives this description of Socrates' final hours. Socrates said to his followers: "There is one way, then, in which a man can be free from all anxiety about the fate of his soul—if in life he has abandoned bodily pleasures and adornments . . . and has devoted himself to the pleasures of acquiring knowledge, and so by decking his soul not with a borrowed beauty but with its own— with self-control, and goodness, and courage, and liberality, and truth—has fitted himself to await his journey to the next world."[14]

It was nearly sunset when the prison officer arrived and told Socrates that it was time for the execution. The officer himself was in tears. Socrates bathed, said goodbye to his children and wife, and sent them home. He then sent his servant to get the executioner. The executioner delivered a cup of prepared poison, a concoction of hemlock. Socrates offered a prayer to the gods. Then, he downed the drink. His friends wept brokenheartedly. Socrates scolded: "Really,

The Death of Socrates, a 1787 painting by Jacques-Louis David, shows Socrates surrounded by his friends and students just before his execution. Although his friends are overcome by grief, Socrates appears calm and dignified as he accepts the cup of poison.

my friends, what a way to behave! Why that was my main reason for sending away the women, to prevent this sort of disturbance, because I am told that one should make one's end in a tranquil frame of mind. Calm yourselves and try to be brave."[15]

The friends composed themselves. Gradually Socrates' feet and then legs went cold and numb. The coldness spread through his body and Socrates spoke his last words, "Crito, we ought to offer a cock to Aesclepius. See to it and don't forget."[16]

That, explained Phaedo, "was the end of our comrade, who was, we may fairly say, of all those whom we knew in our time, the bravest and also the wisest and most upright man."[17]

Socrates' final request to Crito was that he sacrifice a chicken to Asclepius. Asclepius was the god of healing. Greeks made sacrifices to Asclepius to thank him for healing them. Socrates was apparently thanking Asclepius for delivering him to life after death.[18]

THE ACADEMY

PLATO WAS ALMOST THIRTY YEARS OLD when Socrates was executed. Soon after, Plato was reportedly in Megara—a polis west of Athens. One of Socrates' other followers, Euclid of Megara, lived there. After Socrates' death, Plato traveled for several years. He may have performed his military service during part of this time.[1] According to Diogenes Laertius, Plato went to Libya where he met with a mathematician named Theodorus. He also visited Egypt and spent time in Sicily.

Pythagoreans

During his travels, Plato spent time studied with the Pythagoreans in Italy. These were followers of Pythagoras of Samos, a mysterious and influential figure in Greek intellectual history. Pythagoras had moved to Croton, a Greek city in Italy, between 535 B.C. and 525 B.C.—more than a century before Plato's visit. With his followers, he founded a society there. With initiations and passwords, there was a secretive aspect to their society. The Pythagoreans believed that the soul could transmigrate—move from one body to another—after death.

Pythagoreans were especially interested in mathematical inquiry. They believed that "all things are number."[2] The theorem that expresses the relationship between the lengths of sides of a right triangle is known as the Pythagorean Theorem. It can be expressed as $a^2 + b^2 = c^2$. It states that the sum of the squares of the two legs of a right triangle equals the square of the hypotenuse.

Pythagoreans are also credited with discovering mathematical ratios that explain harmonies of musical notes. Plucking the strings of a lyre, for example, it was evident that strings of different lengths produced different pitches. If the length of the string of a low note was reduced to half its original length, they noted, it produced a note one octave higher. The Pythagoreans considered music a sister science of arithmetic, geometry, and astronomy.[3] Influence of the Pythagoreans' mathematical approach is evident in some of Plato's thoughts about the ordered universe.

Life at the Academy

Home again in Athens around 385 B.C., Plato began meeting with other thinkers and young men interested in philosophy. While Socrates had often met with men in the agora, Plato's main meeting place was a short distance outside Athens' city wall. According to Athenian lore, this park-like area had been part of the estate of Academos. In Greek myths, Academos had once helped rescue a kidnapped young girl named Helen; she grew up to be Helen of Troy, whose kidnapping caused the Trojan War. Because of Plato's choice of a place to teach, Academos' name lives on. Plato's school was known as the Academy. Today, an academy is an institution of higher learning or a society for the advancement of art or science.

We do not know what Plato's Academy looked like. In the mild Greek climate, Plato and his associates may have first met outdoors in the shade of olive trees that are known to have grown there. A public gymnasium was located in the area. Gymnasiums were centers of exercise and socializing for men in ancient Greece. They

Plato's Academy was located outside of the Dipylon Gate, one of the main entrances to the center of ancient Athens. Today, the location of the road is marked by signs, nestled along modern streets.

evolved into centers of education. Plato owned land and built or bought a house in this area. His house and gardens may have served as the Academy's campus. A shrine to the Muses was associated with the Academy.[4] The Muses were goddesses of music, poetry, arts, and sciences.

While Plato's Academy is now thought of as a school, it was not like a modern college or university. Students did not take courses taught by professors and earn grades and degrees. No fees were charged to study there. The Academy was more of a community of intellectuals—a place where men met and investigated a range of subjects.[5] It may have been like a club with junior and senior members, where younger men learned from more seasoned thinkers. Teaching probably occurred mostly as informal discussions.

Plato likely guided inquiries by suggesting subjects for consideration. Some of his dialogues were read or performed there. One account tells of a reading of his *Phaedo*. It reports that most of the audience left before the reading was finished. Only Aristotle stayed to the end.[6]

The illustration depicts Plato lecturing at the Academy.

Aristotle shed a little more light on Plato's teaching. He commented on a public lecture given by Plato on the subject of "the Good." This was not a written dialogue, but a lecture that was open to a wider audience than the members of the Academy.

In the *Republic*, Plato described a plan for higher education of future leaders. He recommended ten years of mathematics followed by five years of dialectic, a dialogue type of argument. After these basics, rising thinkers were to have another fifteen years of practical experience.[7] Although it has been suggested that Plato used this model in the Academy, how many young Greek men would have committed to thirty years of education?

In a short time Plato's Academy was attracting thinkers from other parts of Greece. Aristotle, a young man from Stagira in northern Greece arrived at the Academy around 367 B.C. Aristotle studied there for twenty years. Along with Plato, Aristotle is seen as one of the most influential thinkers of all time. Other students of the Academy also made valuable contributions to the development of mathematics and science.

As shown in the *Republic,* Plato believed that mathematics was valuable in helping train the mind. Supposedly a sign at the Academy entrance read, "Let no man unversed in geometry enter." Reports of that sign, though, date from almost one thousand years after Plato lived.[8]

One source of information about the Academy is an account of its history that was written on papyrus in the first century B.C. Although only a few sentences are preserved, they confirm the Academy's emphasis on mathematics. The papyrus mentions *metrologia,* a theory of ratios. Instruction in geometry and mechanics were also noted.[9]

Ancient sources report that Plato assigned geometry problems to his associates and students. A famous one was known as the Delian problem. This problem dealt with a cube-shaped sacrificial altar, dedicated to the god Apollo, on the sanctuary island Delos. Apollo reportedly wanted a bigger altar. The new altar was also to be a cube, but with exactly twice the volume of the first altar. The problem is not easily solved. Suppose the first altar was a one-meter cube. By simply doubling the sides, the cube would have a volume of eight cubic meters (2 x 2 x 2 = 8). Geometers of Plato's time did find the solution.

In another problem, Plato asked his associates and students to determine what uniform and ordered motion could explain the observed paths of the planets through the skies.[10] This problem shows Plato's interest in mathematics to describe natural phenomena.

Many talented Greek mathematicians were connected to the Academy over the years. Their work contributed to the advancement of mathematics. Plato, however, was not an important mathematician. His organized way of thinking and defining terms is similar to the approach that Greeks began to apply to geometry. In Plato's writings he emphasized the importance of definitions of terms. His insistence on definitions and his step-by-step approach to solving problems may have influenced the way geometers of the time began to set out conjectures and proofs.

Some empirical science was also studied at the Academy, even though Plato's priority was abstract knowledge. Empirical means based on observation or derived from experience. A scene from a comic play of Plato's time shows the Academy students making observations. In the scene, Plato and

Although archaeologists have confirmed the site of Plato's Academy, it has not been extensively excavated. The area where Plato once taught and met with fellow thinkers is now a city park.

others are examining a pumpkin. They earnestly inspect it and describe it as a round vegetable, or perhaps a tree, or grass. Showing his amusement at the philosophers' deliberations, the playwright had a character walk past the thinkers and loudly pass gas. The students only briefly paused and then resumed their pumpkin study.[11]

Plato's Academy continued for nine centuries. Teaching and ideas there changed considerably over the years. Plato's school had a remarkable influence in nurturing intellectual thought in the ancient world.

Plato's Writings

Plato, unlike Socrates, was a writer. Socrates taught through conversation. Plato met and talked with students and fellow thinkers; he also wrote philosophical works. Remarkably, all of Plato's known writings still exist today. A few works falsely credited to him have also survived the centuries, attached to his own texts.

Most of Plato's works are dialogues, conversations between two or more characters.

The *Apology*, Plato's version of Socrates' defense at his trial, is a speech, not a dialogue. The *Menexenus* is a funeral speech. Thirteen letters are also part of the Platonic collection, but these are probably not authentic.

Widespread literacy was still relatively new in Plato's time. Private schools taught reading and writing to boys whose families could afford to pay for schools. Some women could read. Writing in the fifth century B.C. was used in government. Laws were sometimes inscribed on public monuments. With writing, spoken words could be stored and read by people who had not been present when the words were uttered. Poems like Homer's epics the *Iliad* and the *Odyssey* had previously been passed on through memorization of thousands of lines. Written down, those lines were preserved for future readers. Written documents could be studied and analyzed by readers. This improved access to information contributed to advances in science.[12]

In Plato's time, books were not like our modern volumes. Papyrus, a paper-like material made from reeds, was made in long narrow sheets. These were stored as rolls. In Plato's time the Greek alphabet had only uppercase letters. Greeks did not put spaces between words and they used no punctuation. Written works were read out loud at shops in the agora. If a customer wanted to purchase a text, he would order it and pay to have it copied.[13] Scribes, possibly slaves, would then copy the work by hand, with ink on papyrus.

Some scholars have suggested that Plato's dialogues were composed to be read out loud. Perhaps they were presented as performances with different men reading the different characters' parts. The question-and-answer format of the dialogues is effective in laying out rational arguments and eliminating unfounded ideas. Many of the dialogues are conversations between friends. As the men stay up all night talking or sit in the garden, the reader is drawn into the conversation. Plato's dialogue style includes the reader in the debate.

Plato himself does not appear in the dialogues.

Socrates, Glaucon, Timaeus, and others participate in the debates, conversations, and speeches. Therefore, Plato never actually states his own opinion on the many subjects addressed. The reader is left to determine which argument or position to accept. Plato sought to stimulate thought, not to just teach lessons about his views.[14]

The exact order and dating of Plato's works is unknown. Traditionally they are organized into three groups: the early, middle, and late dialogues. The early works are also called the Socratic dialogues. Scholars consider these as most influenced by the historic Socrates. With more interaction between the characters than some of the later works, these are more dramatic.

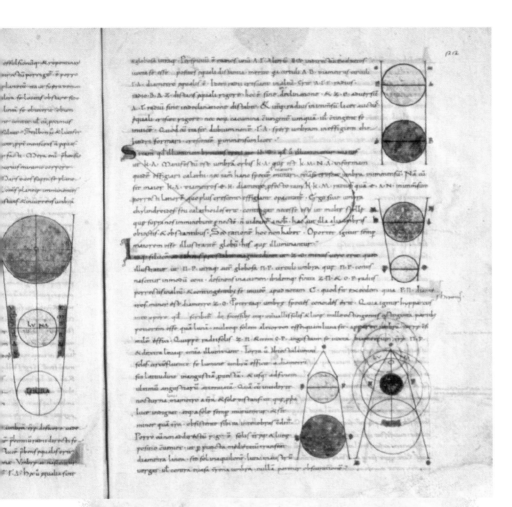

A fourth-century Christian named Calcidius translated Plato's Timaeus into Latin. Here are two pages from a medieval copy of his work.

In these, guided by Socrates' questioning, the characters discuss virtue. Often, Socrates' questions expose the ignorance of those who pretend to have knowledge of qualities like justice or courage. This group of texts includes the *Apology, Charmides, Crito, Euthyphro, Gorgias, Hippias Minor, Ion, Laches,* and *Protagoras.*[15]

In the middle dialogues, Plato seems to offer more of his own philosophy. He puts forth ideas of the just person and just society. Plato's Forms feature in some of these dialogues. Plato's Forms are abstract ideas. The middle dialogues include the *Republic, Symposium, Meno, Phaedo,* and *Cratylus.*[16]

Plato's later dialogues deal more with investigations of society and study of the soul. These include the *Critias, Philebus, Sophist,* and *Statesman.*[17] Plato's main work about cosmology, the *Timaeus,* is also considered a late work. In most of these, the character Socrates plays a small role, or even none at all.

Some of Plato's dialogues were circulated while he was still alive. It is likely that there was an

"Academy edition" of Plato's writing, the official copy at his school and used by his associates.[18] In the centuries after his death his works were copied and studied by generations of thinkers.

Plato's dialogues stimulate thought. They inspire us to think about order in the universe, the human soul, and man's place in nature. Plato tackled great problems. His writings have gloriously endured the centuries and are still relevant and engaging.

5

THEORY OF FORMS

TODAY WHEN WE THINK OF SCIENTIFIC inquiry, our approach often starts with observations and gathering of empirical data. "Empirical" data is information gathered from observation, experience, or experiment. In science classes in school we conduct experiments to gather empirical information.

For example, when we measure the time it takes marbles to roll down tracks of different slopes, we are gathering empirical data. We repeat the experiment several times and collect sets of observations. These may include the length of each track, the track's slope, and the time it takes for the marble to roll a measured distance.

Empirical observation began to be used in

some ancient Greeks' inquiries shortly before Plato's time. Certain Greek physicians kept detailed lists of observations of patients. Through their observations they could see how diseases progressed with different patients. They could use that information to predict how a patient's condition was likely to worsen or improve. Aristotle, a longtime student at Plato's Academy, made great contributions to the study of living things through his empirical observations of animals.

With today's understanding of the value of observations in scientific inquiry, some of Plato's ideas can seem quite unscientific. In Plato's search for knowledge, he did not look for answers in the things perceived by our senses. Instead, he looked for the abstract ideas that he believed explained the things we perceive. Plato was seeking the reality behind the material world. He looked for ideas that could be grasped by the reasoning mind, even though the ideas themselves could not be touched or observed.

Eidos

Plato's word for the underlying reality was *eidos,* usually translated as "form."[1] His exploration of this subject is known as Plato's Theory of Forms. If Plato had written "An Introduction to the Forms," questions that have puzzled thinkers for centuries might have been answered. Part of the joy of studying Plato, though, is that he leads the reader to think. Plato's Forms are not laid out in one single dialogue. They recur in works such as the *Republic, Phaedo, Timaeus, Symposium,* and *Statesman*. Making them even more elusive, the Forms seem to have different meanings in different dialogues. Plato may have revised his thinking about them through the years.[2]

The physical world, Plato saw, was in perpetual flux; it was always changing.[3] Changeable objects, he believed, could not be objects of true knowledge. Seeking knowledge, he wanted to find things that were always true. He suggested that there were Forms that existed in a different way than the things perceived by our senses.

One way to approach Plato's Forms is through

mathematics. Mathematics, Plato wrote, "has a great power of leading the mind upwards and forcing it to reason about pure numbers, refusing to discuss collections of material things which can be seen and touched."[4] Plato recognized that objects in mathematics, like numbers and geometric shapes, exist in a different way than physical objects. They are real objects that are understood by the mind, but are not "seen or touched."[5]

From our own experiences, we can get an introduction to Plato's meaning. From an early age, most of us know our numbers and understand some basic arithmetic. We know, for example that two plus three equals five. If we have two potatoes and add three more potatoes to them, we know that we have a total of five potatoes. This addition will also be true if we add two pianos and three pianos. The potatoes and pianos are material objects, but the underlying truth is that two plus three equals five. We also know that the numbers "two" and "three" are not potatoes or pianos. If you take the potatoes or pianos away, the mathematical objects "two" and "three" still exist. Plato was saying that the study of mathematics can train the mind from earthly objects to abstract thinking. Numbers, unlike the potatoes or pianos, are unchanging. "Two" itself does not change, even though it can be applied to a limitless number of material things or nonmaterial ideas.

Similar to the objects of mathematics, Plato believed that there were Forms for ideas. Equality, beauty, justice, and "the Good" had Forms.[6] Plato also wrote about Forms for physical things. In the *Cratylus,* Socrates talked with a young man about Forms. As an example, Socrates used a shuttle. A shuttle is a tool used by weavers to pass a thread through rows of lengthwise threads. To the Greeks, a shuttle was a familiar object.

> Socrates: And suppose the shuttle is broken in making. Will he make another according to the broken one? Or will he look to the form according to which he made the other?
>
> Hermogenes: To the latter I should imagine.
>
> Socrates: Might not that be justly called the true or ideal shuttle?

Hermogenes: I think so.

Socrates: And whatever shuttles are wanted, for the manufacture of garments, thin or thick, of flaxen, woolen, or other material, ought all of them have the true form of the shuttle, and whatever is the shuttle best adapted to each kind of work, that ought to be the form which the maker produces in each case?[7]

Plato's idea of the Form of the shuttle is its pattern or design. The ideal shuttle to weave wool, for example, is not one specific physical shuttle— it is the plan that can be used to make an infinite number of wool shuttles. In Plato's scheme, individual shuttles "participate" in the Form. They have the shuttle Form's characteristics, but are

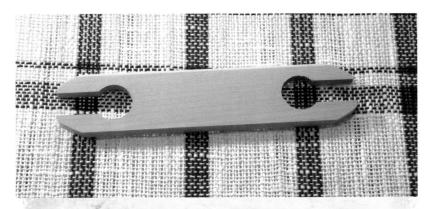

A shuttle (above) is a device used in weaving to pass the weft thread between the warp threads. In explaining the Forms, Plato used the example of a shuttle.

made of matter. The physical shuttle will change with time. It may break or burn or just get worn down. During the physical shuttle's existence, it "participates" in the qualities of the Form.

Plato wrote that the Forms were eternal; they were timeless and always existed. They also had no material existence of their own. How then did these Forms relate to our physical world? Plato suggested that there was a divine creator of the universe. This creator was not one of the Greek gods like Zeus or Athena. The creator, Plato asserted, made the heavens, Earth, and all things according to an order or plan. Things that we see and touch, he believed, were made from available material and were imperfect compared to their Forms.[8]

The Allegory of the Cave

To Plato, true knowledge was not of material things but of the Forms, the underlying abstract truths. In the *Republic*, Plato presented views of justice and just communities. Plato believed that the leaders of a polis should be wise. Leaders should be men who used their intellect.[9] In the *Republic,* he suggested education to help potential leaders cultivate wisdom. The purpose of their training was to guide their minds away from the material world of their senses to understand a higher abstract realm. To illustrate the importance of this higher understanding, Plato's Socrates told a type of story called an allegory. An allegory is a story in which people, things, and actions represent an idea about life. Socrates began: "Imagine the condition of men living in a sort of cavernous chamber underground. . . . Here they have been from childhood, chained by the leg and also by the neck, so that they cannot move and can see only what is in front of them, because the chains will not let them turn their heads."[10]

Plato explained that behind these men a fire was burning. They could not see it because of their chains. Between the fire and the men was a stage. When models of objects were moved across the stage, light from the fire projected their shadows on the wall in front of the prisoners. The objects

In Plato's Allegory of the Cave, prisoners can only see shadows projected on a wall and believe these illusions to be reality. In the cave, the prisoners cannot see the objects that are carried in front of the fire that cast the shadows.

were not the real things—they were copies, like a wooden pitcher or a stuffed dog.

If Plato was alive today, he might set this scene in a movie theater.[11] The audience members, chained in seats would only see the films projected on the screen. The characters and places in the movies would seem real to them. Suppose that they only saw cartoons. That cartoon world would be the only world known to the prisoners. As Socrates said in the allegory, "such prisoners would recognize as reality nothing but the shadows of those artificial objects."[12]

In the dialogue, Socrates considered what would happen if one man was released: "Suppose one of them set free and forced suddenly to stand up, turn his head and walk with eyes lifted to the light. . . .What do you think he would say if someone told him that what he had formerly seen was meaningless illusion, but now, being somewhat nearer to reality and turned toward more real objects, he was getting a truer view? Suppose further that he were shown the objects being carried by. . . .Would he not be perplexed and believe the objects now shown him to be not so real as what he formerly saw?"[13]

The prisoner would probably be confused and not believe that the objects had caused the shadows. After this experience, Plato then continued the story as the prisoner was dragged outside into the sunlight: "At first it would be easiest to make out shadows, and then the images of men and things reflected in water and later on the things themselves. After that it would be easier to look at the heavenly bodies and the sky itself by night. . . . Last of all he would be able to look at the sun and contemplate its nature, not as it appears when reflected in water or any alien medium, but as it is in itself in its own domain."[14]

The Allegory of the Cave, Plato wrote, is about the journey of the human soul from ignorance to knowledge. The cave prison "corresponds to the region revealed to us through the sense of sight." The sense of sight, though, did not reveal the truth:

> The ascent to see the things in the upper world you may take as standing for the upward journey of the soul into the region of the intelligible. . . . In the world of knowledge the last thing to be perceived and only with great difficulty is the essential Form of Goodness. Once it is perceived, the conclusion must follow that, for all things this is the cause of whatever is right and good. . . . Without having had a vision of this Form no one can act with wisdom, either in his own life or in matters of state.[15]

The Allegory of the Cave shows us several aspects of Plato's thought. We see in it his view that there is a Form of "the Good." Having understanding of this Form of goodness is essential to wisdom. Leaders of governments should have wisdom, knowledge of this ideal good, Plato believed. He recognized that time and effort would be required to move from knowledge derived from physical experience to the higher intellectual realm. Elsewhere in the *Republic*, he writes more about how leaders can be trained to think philosophically and move to understanding the Form of "the Good."

The allegory also clearly shows us Plato's view that relying on our senses does not reveal wisdom. The prisoners' senses showed them only a world of shadows. Our senses, he seems to be saying, are like chains that hold us down and keep us from true knowledge.[16]

How Plato's Forms relate to scientific thought can be viewed in different ways. Some scholars have considered Plato an enemy of science who rejected understanding of the material world. A different view is that his ideas of abstract truths are indeed relevant to science. In this view, Plato's thinking was similar to modern scientists who look for the abstract laws that lie behind empirical data.[17]

At the beginning of this chapter we considered a science class experiment with marbles rolled down tracks of different slopes. The purpose of the experiment was not just to see how far or fast an individual marble rolled. The goal of the experiment was to learn about momentum, the product of an object's mass and velocity. Momentum is described in mathematical terms. Careful measurements from a systematic series of experiments can provide data for calculating momentum. Like one of Plato's Forms, momentum is an abstract concept. It exists apart from specific concrete objects. Momentum is evidence that a force has acted upon a mass.

Centuries after Plato, science took a giant leap forward when thinkers began setting up experiments to collect observations in an organized way. The combination of experiment, observation, and mathematics proved to be a stunningly fruitful approach to learning about the natural world. As modern science charged forward, instruments like clocks, telescopes, and microscopes helped scientists observe and measure more accurately than their unaided senses permitted.

Thanks to years of research and applications of mathematical abstractions to physical problems, today we know many scientific laws that describe and predict natural phenomena. Laws of motion, conservation laws, and gas laws are a few of them. These laws do not exist as physical things themselves, but are observed in objects and matter. Many of them are expressed as mathematical statements. These natural laws were not discovered through reason alone, as Plato seemed to recommend. However, as thinkers explore abstractions of mathematics and find patterns and relationships, their discoveries sometimes suggest experiments and reveal connections in the physical world. With Plato's enthusiasm for abstractions and mathematics, we can wonder how he would see his Forms in today's science.

6

COSMOLOGY

"LET ME PROCEED TO EXPLAIN TO YOU Socrates, the order in which we have arranged our entertainment. Our intention is that Timaeus, who is the most of an astronomer among us, and has made the nature of the universe his special study, should speak first, beginning with the generation of the world and going down to the creation of man," says Critias.[1]

Critias, a friend of Socrates, is introducing the topic of the *Timaeus*, Plato's only work that focuses on the natural world. Plato's view of the organization of Earth, the sun, moon, planets, and stars is presented in it. In his cosmic model, movements of the heavens can be described in mathematical terms. The *Timaeus* includes an explanation of matter, which is also described through mathematics.

Plato considered the material world to be imperfect, not perfect like the abstract realm of the Forms. Even though they fell short of the ideal, he thought that our world and universe are the best they can possibly be.[2] Studying them could be a pleasant recreation, he wrote. For Plato, the goal of an exercise like observing the stars was not to learn about the specific physical things themselves, but to learn about the rational order behind them. The purpose of these investigations should be to "seek for the divine in all things, as far as our nature admits."[3] Plato's objective in studying the natural world is to get closer to understanding the abstract.

The *Timaeus* is widely believed to be one of Plato's later works. Timaeus, a friend of Socrates, is the chief speaker. He gives a detailed account of the creation and organization of the cosmos. The Greek word *kosmos* meant, among other things, "orderly arrangement." The cosmos is the universe and everything in it. The *Timaeus* shows us questions that Greek thinkers considered in the early days of philosophy and scientific inquiry. They wondered what things were made of and how to explain change. They sought explanations for the apparent movements of the sun, moon, and other heavenly bodies. They wondered how the universe began and how humankind fit into the great cosmic picture.

Plato's Demiurge and Model of the Universe

Early in the *Timaeus,* Plato explains that the universe was laid out according to a plan, a higher abstract idea, like the Forms. According to Plato, that was accomplished by a Demiurge— the Greek word for craftsman. Plato's Demiurge is the personification of reason.[4]

"Now that which is created must . . . of necessity be created by a cause. . . . This question, however, we must ask about the world. Which of the patterns had the artificer [Demiurge] in mind when he made it—the pattern of the unchangeable or of that which is created? . . .

Everyone will see that he must have looked to the eternal, for the world is the fairest of creations and he is the best of causes. And having been created in this way, the world has been framed in the likeness of that which is apprehended by reason and mind and is unchangeable, and must therefore . . . be a copy of something."[5]

The craftsman wanted his creation to be as good as possible, so he used the best plan for it. The world is good in resembling the craftsman's plan.[6] Like the Forms, this plan was eternal and did not have a physical existence of its own. Plato's Demiurge, unlike creators in many religions, did not create the material of the universe. He worked with unformed material that already existed.[7]

Plato wrote that the Demiurge used mathematical principles in building the cosmos. As we saw with the Forms, mathematical objects do not exist in the same way as physical objects. Even so, they are intelligible and can be understood by the mind. Unlike the physical world that is in flux, numbers and other mathematical objects are unchanging. To understand the order of the cosmos and the Forms, Plato seems to be saying, one needs to know its mathematical basis.[8]

In Plato's model, Earth stood at the center of a spherical universe. Earth itself was a sphere. The moon, sun, planets, and stars revolved around it, following circular paths:

> First there was the moon in the orbit nearest the Earth, and next the sun in the second orbit above the Earth; then came the morning star [Venus] and the star said to be sacred to Hermes [Mercury], moving in orbits which have an equal swiftness with the sun but in an opposite direction. . . . To enumerate the places which he assigned to the other stars and to give all the reasons why he assigned them, although a secondary matter, would give more trouble than the primary. These things at some future time when we are at leisure.[9]

Today we know that the planets, including Earth, revolve around the sun. The ancient Greeks did not have that perspective. However, they were familiar with observed movement of heavenly bodies. They knew the observed annual path of the sun. Living in a world without artificial lighting, they saw thousands of twinkling stars in the night sky. They saw that the stars seemed to move together, as though fixed on a huge

Schema huius præmissæ diuisionis Sphærarum.

In the *Timaeus*, Plato described the universe as Earth-centered and asserted that it was laid out with reason. This idea of a spherical cosmos with heavenly bodies moving in circular paths was refined by Aristotle and later by Ptolemy. The Earth-centered model of the universe was widely accepted into the sixteenth century.

sphere. Some objects in the night sky did not move with the stars, but slowly traced individual paths through the heavens. They called these "wanderers." The Greek word for wanderer is the root of our word "planet." Five planets are visible to the naked eye—without use of a telescope—Mercury, Venus, Mars, Jupiter, and Saturn. "Now by reason of motion of the same, those which revolved fastest appeared to be overtaken by those which moved slower although they really overtook them, for the motion of the same made them all turn in a spiral. . . . That there might be some visible measure of their relative swiftness and slowness as they proceeded in their eight courses, God lighted a fire which we now call the sun, in the second from the Earth of these orbits, that it might give light to the whole of heaven."[10]

For a man who was not particularly interested in the physical realm or the use of observation in understanding nature, Plato showed considerable familiarity with observations of heavenly bodies. He recognized that the observed movements of the planets could be explained by combinations of circular motions.[11]

The model that Plato described was refined by Aristotle and a later Greek astronomer named Ptolemy. Another Greek thinker, Aristarchus, suggested that the sun was at the center of the cosmos. Earth, Aristarchus proposed, revolved around the sun. His idea found few followers at the time. The Earth-centered, spherical universe was the accepted cosmology throughout Europe for almost two thousand years.

Platonic Solids

According to Plato, the matter that the Demiurge used for the cosmos was pre-existing. The Demiurge did not create matter—he rearranged it. He took the pre-existing chaotic material, and arranged it with reason and order, at least with as much reason and order as physical matter could be shaped.

Plato's Demiurge made the world and its living and nonliving things from four elements. These were the elements of early Greek science—fire,

Atlantis

"Now in this island of Atlantis, there was a great and wonderful empire which had rule over the whole island and several others," explained Critias in Plato's *Timaeus*. Long ago, the people of Atlantis tried to conquer Athens, he said. The Athenians, with virtue, strength, courage, and military skill, magnificently defeated the invaders. After the confrontation, there were "violent earthquakes and floods, and in a single day and night of misfortune . . . the island of Atlantis . . . disappeared in the depths of the sea."[12]

Plato's dialogues provide the earliest existing accounts of the legendary lost island of Atlantis. He introduces the island briefly in the *Timaeus*. The purpose of the story of Atlantis is actually to show how an ideal state, like the one described in the *Republic*, would fight in a war. In the *Critias*, Plato describes Atlantis in vibrant detail.

According to Critias, Poseidon, the god of the sea, laid out the island. At the center of Atlantis was a mountain. Beyond it were "alternate rings of sea and land . . . he fashioned two such round wheels, as we may call them, of earth and three of sea." Poseidon divided the lands between ten brothers—five pairs of twins. Critias describes the palace with golden statues of winged horses and dolphins, a grove with all kinds of trees, gardens, temples, gymnasiums, a racecourse for horse races. Atlantis was an island of abundance and riches, and for a long time the Atlanteans had happy lives. Eventually, though, "the human temper [began] to predominate, then they . . . began to behave themselves unseemly. To the seeing eye they now began to seem foul, for they were losing the fairest bloom from their most precious treasure. . . . [T]hey were taking the infection of wicked coveting and pride of power."[13] The *Critias* stops abruptly, shortly after this statement. Zeus is about to lay a judgement on the people of Atlantis.

Atlantis has captured imaginations for centuries. Plato's story has been embellished and retold, even made the subject of movies. Scholars have studied Plato's *Timaeus* and *Critias*. Historians have considered whether there might be any factual basis for the tale of the lost island.

South of Athens in the Aegean Sea is an area of considerable geologic activity. Around the seventeenth century B.C., a massive volcanic eruption devastated an island group now known as Santorini. Most of the land in its center sank when the volcano's magma chamber collapsed. Pumice and ash covered what remained of the island. Archaeologists have excavated part of a town, now known as Akrotiri, that was buried by the volcanic debris. Houses decorated with beautiful wall paintings, streets and squares, and even a public water system have been uncovered. Akrotiri is identified with the Minoan civilization. The Minoan civilization was centered on the island of Crete from around 2700 B.C. to 1450 B.C. Archaeologists have suggested that Plato's Atlantis story is connected to Santorini.

air, earth, and water. Plato believed that they existed in mathematical proportion.

Plato explained: "As fire is to air so is air to water, and as air is to water so is water to Earth— and thus he bound and put together a visible and tangible heaven. And for these reasons, and out of such elements which are in number four, the body of the world was created, and it was harmonized by proportion, and therefore has the spirit of friendship."[14]

Fire, earth, air, and water made up the matter of Plato's universe. Rocks, oceans, olive trees, the marble columns of the Parthenon, the wooden ships of the Athenian fleet, men and women, clouds, coins, grapes—all the things of the Greeks' world were made from combinations of elements in various proportions. To Plato, on an even more fundamental level, the elements were made of mathematical ingredients.[15] He identified each element with a shape.

In Plato's time and today, there are five, and only five, convex regular polyhedra. (A polyhedron is a solid figure bounded by many plane figures.) These are the tetrahedron, cube, octahedron, icosahedron, and dodecahedron. In each of these five solids, all edges, faces, and angles are equal. The cube, for example, is formed of six squares whose edges meet at 90-degree angles. The tetrahedron is comprised of four equilateral triangles. *Tetra* means four. The dodecahedron is comprised of twelve, *dodeca,* pentagons—five -sided polygons. Because of the *Timaeus,* these five solids are known as the Platonic solids, named for Plato. He did not discover them. They were already known to geometry-minded Greeks. He may have studied them with the Pythagoreans when he was in Italy.

These solids have intrigued mathematicians through the ages. In his cosmology, Plato associated these shapes with elements. Fire, he said, was the small sharp tetrahedron. Air was the octahedron. Water was the icosahedron. The element earth was the cube. The dodecahedron, the figure closest to the sphere, he identified with the whole universe—the shape of the Demiurge's creation.[16]

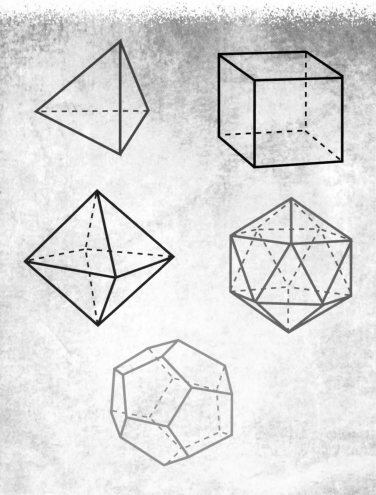

These five shapes, known as Platonic solids, are regular polyhedra. In each figure, all faces are equal, angles are equal, edges are equal, and vertices are equal. The tetrahedron has four triangular faces. The cube has six square faces. The octahedron has eight triangular faces. The dodecahedron has twelve pentagonal faces. The icosahedron has twenty triangular faces.

Plato went a step further with his elements and geometry. The faces of four of the solids, all but the dodecahedron, could be further broken down into two types of triangles. Right-angled isosceles and half-equilateral triangles could be arranged to make the triangular and square faces of the figures.[17] In this way of thinking, the Demiurge had made the cosmos out of triangles.

One of the recurring questions in early Greek science was how to explain change. For example, how could a log burn and become ash—a totally different substance than its original wood? In Plato's model, if the elements were really triangles, then their combinations could change according to mathematical formulas. With Plato's theory, the triangles that made up the elements could combine to change elements or compounds. Triangles in water, for example, were arranged in icosahedra. If the water was boiled, the triangles could rearrange into octahedra of air and tetrahedra of fire.[18]

With refinements from Aristotle and later Ptolemy, Plato's model of the Earth-centered

Plato identified the Greeks' four elements with the regular polyhedra. He explained their construction in terms of triangles. A square can be made with four identical right-angled isosceles triangles. An equilateral triangle can be made with six identical half-equilateral triangles.

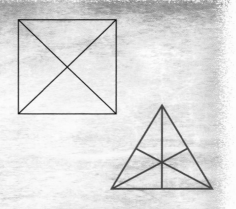

cosmos was the European view of the universe for nearly two thousand years. In 1543, Nicolaus Copernicus published a book suggesting that the sun, rather than Earth, might be at the center of our system. Soon after, using a newly invented optical device, the telescope, Galileo looked at the heavens. Through his telescope, Galileo saw moons revolving around the planet Jupiter. Like Plato and other Greek philosophers, these thinkers looked for rational explanations for the order of the cosmos. If a force existed to allow moons to orbit Jupiter, Galileo surmised, that same force could allow Earth to orbit the sun. Soon after Galileo's ideas were published, Johannes Kepler studied hundreds of observations to make sense of planets' observed movements. Kepler looked to mathematics for his answer and found that the planets follow elliptical paths around the sun.

In 1687, Isaac Newton published his *Philosophiae Naturalis Principia Mathematicae,* Mathematical Principles of Natural Philosophy. In it he stated three laws of motion. Taken together, these describe the gravitational attraction between bodies with mass. They explain why planets stay in orbit around the sun; why satellites, including

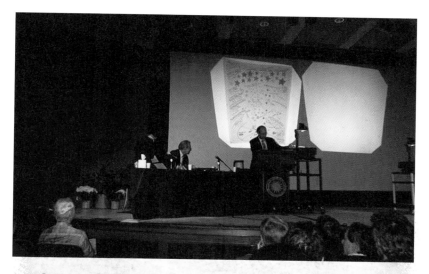

Scientists today study the large-scale geometry of the universe. At the 1998 Nature of the Universe Debate in Washington, D.C., scientists presented academic papers on theories about the matter and density of the universe.

the moon, stay in orbit around Earth; and why dropped objects fall down. Like Plato, Newton used mathematics to describe the physical world. Unlike Plato, Newton used detailed observations and experiments—study of the physical world— to find the abstract ideas underlying physical phenomena.

Through the centuries since Plato wrote the *Timaeus*, there have been remarkable scientific advances. Today, with powerful telescopes we see distant galaxies, with spacecraft we photograph the surfaces of other planets, and with particle accelerators we study subatomic particles. Like Plato, we are still seeking understanding of the order of the universe. Much scientific study is based on empirical observation. Yet modern science also includes theoretical investigations, studies that use mathematical models and abstractions of physics to try explain natural phenomena. As scientists study quantum physics, microquasars, the curvature of spacetime, and more, their research recalls Plato's approach.

LEGACY

FROM THE TIME PLATO STARTED THE Academy around 385 B.C., he spent most of the rest of his life in Athens. Mathematician and philosopher friends and colleagues came to the Academy. Their names are not well known to us today, but men including Eudoxus of Cnidus, Theaetetus, and Menaechmus who made contributions to the development of mathematics were among his circle. As Socrates had followers and friends in inquiry, Plato did too.

Plato apparently left Athens twice, to help with leadership changes in Syracuse, a prosperous Greek polis on the island of Sicily. When the ruler of Syracuse died, Plato was invited by a relative of the ruler to help train the young heir to the throne. With Plato's views of training leaders in philosophy, it must have seemed like a fantastic opportunity. However, when he arrived in Sicily, around 365 B.C., the situation was not as conducive to his educational approach as he might have wished. Syracuse was at war. There was also ongoing intrigue about whether Plato was invited to truly train the heir to the throne, or to keep him out of the way.[1] Plato soon returned to Athens.

In 362 B.C., Plato was summoned back to Syracuse. With the ongoing power struggle there, his trip was not successful and he returned home again the next year. By some reports, he was even kidnapped by pirates on the voyage home. The main sources of information about these trips are letters credited to Plato. The letters are probably not authentic, so details from them are not widely accepted.[2]

Plato died in around 347 B.C. He was eighty or eighty-one years old. He had never married and had no children. His nephew, Speusippus, became the new director of the Academy.

Aristotle

At the time of Plato's first trip to Syracuse, a new student, Aristotle, had arrived at the Academy. Aristotle would become as famous as his teacher. He spent twenty years at the school. During his time there he learned about Plato's Forms and his teacher's ideas of a higher realm of abstract ideas. Along with the investigations of mathematics and discussions of ethics and justice, he discussed Plato's cosmology.

After Plato died, Aristotle left Athens for several years. First he moved to the coast of

what is now Turkey and then the island of Lesbos. During these years he conducted research into marine biology. He studied

Aristotle spent twenty years studying at Plato's Academy. This Roman bust of Aristotle is based on Greek sculpture from 330 B.C.

and wrote detailed descriptions of fish, lobsters, octopus, and other marine animals. Aristotle was then summoned to the court of King Philip of Macedon. There, Aristotle supposedly tutored Philip's son, who would grow up to be Alexander the Great. When Alexander was a young man he set out on his military campaigns. Aristotle returned to Athens. Instead of rejoining the Academy, though, he began his own intellectual center. It became known as the Lyceum.

Aristotle was greatly influenced by Plato. Several of Plato's ideas show through in his work. Aristotle's view of the heaven, planets, and Earth was certainly related to his teacher's cosmology. They also had their differences. Plato looked to Forms and abstract ideas to find the order of the cosmos. Aristotle looked to things that could be perceived by the senses. He studied fish, animals, plants, rocks, rivers, and insects. He observed the heavens and their movements. He looked at the physical properties of substances and tried to understand their composition. Where Plato had little interest in empirical data, Aristotle thrived on it. For his studies and inquiries, Aristotle is known as the Father of Empiricism, the Father of Biology, the Father of Zoology, the Father of Logic, and more.

Plato's Influence on Western Philosophy

Discoveries and advances by Aristotle, and other thinkers who studied at the Academy, are part of Plato's legacy. By establishing the Academy and debating and examining subjects with other thinkers, Plato nurtured intellectual pursuits. He set an example of detailed, thoughtful, and rigorous examination of a remarkable range of subjects. Plato's Academy continued for centuries, directed by a continuous line of successors for more than three hundred years. Through the years, teaching there changed a great deal. The school did not even stay in the same location.

Plato's ideas in his remarkable collection of writings shaped western philosophy. "The safest general characterization of the European philosophical tradition is that it consists of a

This volume of Plato's works was published in 1578.

series of footnotes to Plato," wrote philosopher
and mathematician Alfred North Whitehead.[3]

Topics that Plato considered are ones that
we ponder today—goodness, justice, moral
behavior, and our world and universe. As modern
scientists look for rational explanations for
natural phenomena, their inquiries in some ways
resemble Plato's. They still seek abstract ideas
to explain the natural world and they turn to
mathematics to explain its structure.[4]

Reading Plato's works, we can still go on
journeys of inquiry with him and gain new
insights. More than two millennia after Plato
composed his dialogues, his words still stimulate
thought.

ACTIVITIES

Platonic Solids

Plato believed that there was order to the universe and that its movements and structure could be described in mathematical terms. He identified certain geometric shapes with the four elements of the Greeks—fire, air, earth, and water—and the heavenly sphere. There are exactly five of these geometric objects. They are known as the Platonic solids.

The Platonic solids are convex regular polyhedra. *Polyhedra* (the plural of polyhedron) comes from Greek and means "many faces." Each face of one of these solids is a regular polygon, a straight-sided figure with equal sides and equal angles. Every face, angle, and vertex of a regular polyhedron is equal. "Convex" means that the angles project outward rather than inward.

The tetrahedron has four faces; each face is an equilateral triangle. Plato identified the tetrahedron with fire. The octahedron has eight faces; these are also equilateral triangles. Plato identified the octahedron with air. The cube has six faces; each face is a square. Plato identified the cube with the element earth.

You can make these three shapes with the attached pattern.

Materials

- ❖ tracing paper or photocopier
- ❖ tape
- ❖ scissors

Photocopy or trace the diagrams below. You may want to enlarge them. Cut the shapes out and fold along the solid lines. Use small pieces of tape to secure the edges when the figures are folded.

Several Web sites have printable Platonic solids if you would like to make all five shapes.

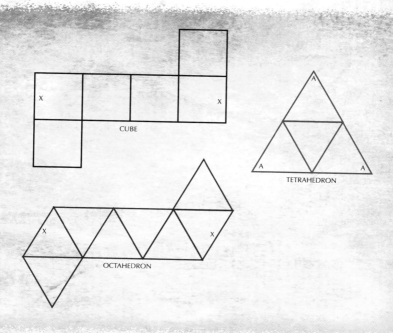

107

Read Plato

Plato has stimulated thought for nearly twenty-four centuries. In his dialogues he examined an extraordinary range of subjects—politics, justice, love, the universe, knowledge, goodness, and more. He asked questions that we still try to answer.

Through this book, you have had a very brief introduction to Plato. Thousands of books have been written about him; countless scholars have spent their careers studying him. Plato is unequaled in philosophy. His thoughts had incredible influence over the centuries.

Reading Plato can be tremendously rewarding. Most school libraries have books about Plato and books with selections of his writings. Many Web sites have his texts online. Plato's style of dialogue invites the reader to have opinions and agree or disagree with the arguments of different characters.

There is no better way to get to know Plato than by reading some of his works yourself. You may want to start with one of his Socratic texts. These are believed to belong to his first stage of writing. They include some lively debates and show Socrates' personality. The *Phaedo* includes the memorable account of Socrates' last hours.

The *Laches* looks at ideas of bravery and courage. The *Symposium,* set at a dinner party, examines love. Plato's *Republic,* examines the just state and the good life, among other things. The *Republic* includes the Allegory of the Cave. The *Timaeus,* a later work, presents Plato's cosmology. His description of Atlantis is found in the *Critias* and *Timaeus*.

Do not be discouraged by Plato's language or confusing ideas. Plato is not read just once and forgotten. Like readers through the centuries, you can return to Plato's writings over and over again.

Observe the Night Sky

The *Timaeus* shows that Plato was familiar with the movements of the sun, moon, planets, and stars. Ancient Greeks knew that some objects in the night sky moved in different paths than the apparent sphere of the stars. They called these five objects "wanderers." The Greek name for them is the root of the English word *planet*.

One of Plato's ideas that connects him with modern science was his belief that the movements of the cosmos could be described in mathematical terms. Today we know that this is true. To understand what perplexing problems the planets posed, you can start observing them yourself.

Five planets, Saturn, Jupiter, Mars, Venus, and Mercury, are visible to the "naked eye." You do not need a telescope to see them. Some newspapers publish daily or weekly star charts with information on the night sky. There are also many Web sites that can help you find planets on any night.

To understand the challenge of describing and predicting the planets' paths, you should make observations over a period of several weeks. You do not need to go out and observe every night. In fact the challenge will be clearer as you see them move over an extended time.

To start your observations, begin on a night with no clouds and preferably without a full moon. From the newspaper or Web site, you will learn what planets are visible that night and where to look in the sky. Find a comfortable place to sit or stand and allow your eyes to adjust to the darkness. In making your observations, you will find that Mercury is the most elusive. Mercury and Venus will always be near the sun. Venus you will find either in the western sky after sunset or the eastern sky before dawn.

When you observe the planets, notice the

stars around them. You can draw a diagram or print a star chart for that day. Be sure to identify the planets on the diagram. About a week later, observe the planets again. Repeat the observations several times, each time recording the planets' positions relative to the background stars. This exercise will help you understand Plato's view of the apparent sphere of the heavens. It will also show that finding mathematical descriptions of the planets' paths from observations taken from a moving planet, Earth, was difficult.

CHRONOLOGY

600–440 B.C.—Approximate dates of the pre-Socratic philosophers, including Thales, Anaximander, and Empedocles.

469 B.C.—Socrates is born.

450–380 B.C.—Sophists teach in Athens.

431–404 B.C.—Peloponnesian War between Athens and Sparta.

428 B.C.—Plato is born. His mother Perictone and his father Ariston were members of aristocratic Athenian families.

423 B.C.—Aristophanes' play *The Clouds* satirizes Socrates and his teaching.

408 B.C.—Plato begins meeting with Socrates around this time.

399 B.C.—Socrates' trial and execution. Plato leaves Athens and travels for several years.

385–380 B.C.—Back in Athens, Plato founds the Academy.

367 B.C.—Aristotle arrives at the Academy and begins twenty years of study there.

365 B.C.—Plato travels to Syracuse to help train heir to the throne.

362 B.C.—Plato again visits Syracuse.

347 B.C.—Plato dies. His nephew Speusippus becomes director of the Academy.

CHAPTER NOTES

Chapter 1. "A Good Talk"

1. Edith Hamilton and Huntington Cairns, eds., *The Collected Dialogues of Plato* (Princeton: Princeton University Press, 1973), pp. 576–577.

2. Ibid., p. 577.

3. T. E. Rihill, *Greek Science* (Oxford: Oxford University Press, 1999), p. 2; Richard Kraut, ed., *The Cambridge Companion to Plato* (New York: Cambridge University Press, 1992), p. 1.

4. G. E. R. Lloyd, *Early Greek Science: Thales to Aristotle* (New York: W.W. Norton and Co., 1970), p. 67.

5. Edward Grant, *A History of Natural Philosophy: From the Ancient World to the Nineteenth Century* (Cambridge: Cambridge University Press, 2007), pp. 23–24.

6. Lloyd, p. 79.

7. Ibid., p. 10.

8. James Longrigg, *Greek Medicine From the Heroic to the Hellenistic Age* (New York: Routledge, 1998), p. 19.

9. Lloyd, pp. 17–18.

10. David C. Lindberg, *The Beginnings of Western Science* (Chicago: University of Chicago Press, 2007), p. 35.

Chapter 2. Son of Athens

1. Diogenes Laertius, *Lives of Eminent Philosophers,* vol. 1 (Cambridge, Mass.: Harvard University Press, 1972), p. 277.

2. Simon Hornblower and Antony Spawforth,

eds., *The Oxford Classical Dictionary* (New York: Oxford University Press, 1996), p. 62.

3. Ibid., p. 507.
4. Diogenes Laertius, p. 279.
5. Ibid., p. 281.
6. Hornblower, p. 452.
7. Ibid., pp. 451–452.
8. Ibid., p. 1415.
9. Ibid.

Chapter 3. Sophists and Socrates

1. Christopher Shields, ed., *The Blackwell Guide to Ancient Philosophy* (Malden, Mass.: Blackwell Publishing, 2003), p. 36.
2. Ibid., p. 28.
3. Simon Hornblower and Antony Spawforth, eds., *The Oxford Classical Dictionary* (New York: Oxford University Press, 1996), p. 1419.
4. Ibid.
5. Richard Kraut, ed., *The Cambridge Companion to Plato* (New York: Cambridge University Press, 1992), p. 3.
6. Paul Cartledge, ed., *The Cambridge Illustrated History of Ancient Greece* (New York: Cambridge University Press, 1998), p. 369.
7. Edith Hamilton and Huntington Cairns, eds., *The Collected Dialogues of Plato* (Princeton: Princeton University Press, 1973), p. 7.
8. Shields, p. 51.
9. Hornblower and Spawforth, p. 451.
10. Ibid.
11. Ibid., p. 1513.
12. Hamilton and Cairns, p. 3.
13. Cartledge, p. 302.
14. Hamilton and Cairns, p. 95.

15. Ibid., p. 97.
16. Ibid., p. 98.
17. Ibid.
18. Ibid., p. 40.

Chapter 4. The Academy

1. *Dictionary of Scientific Biography,* s.v. "Plato."
2. Paul Cartledge, ed., *The Cambridge Illustrated History of Ancient Greece* (New York: Cambridge University Press, 1998), p. 294.
3. Gail Fine, ed., *The Oxford Handbook of Plato* (New York: Oxford University Press, 2008), p. 47.
4. Cartledge, p. 307.
5. Richard Kraut, ed., *The Cambridge Companion to Plato* (New York: Cambridge University Press, 1992), p. 170.
6. Fine, p. 65.
7. Kraut, p. 171.
8. *Dictionary of Scientific Biography,* s.v. "Plato."
9. Kraut, pp. 172–173.
10. Ibid., pp. 173–174.
11. Ibid., pp. 171–172.
12. David C. Lindberg, *The Beginnings of Western Science* (Chicago: University of Chicago Press, 2007), p. 11.
13. Fine, p. 65.
14. Simon Hornblower and Antony Spawforth, eds., *The Oxford Classical Dictionary* (New York: Oxford University Press, 1996), p. 1190.
15. Kraut, p. 5.
16. Ibid., p. 9.
17. Ibid., p. 16.
18. Fine, p. 67.

Chapter 5. Theory of Forms

1. Richard Kraut, ed., *The Cambridge Companion to Plato* (New York: Cambridge University Press, 1992), p. 7.

2. Ibid., pp. 8–9.

3. Edward Grant, *A History of Natural Philosophy: From the Ancient World to the Nineteenth Century* (Cambridge: Cambridge University Press, 2007), p. 23.

4. Francis MacDonald Cornford, trans. and ed., *The Republic of Plato* (Oxford: Oxford University Press, 1972), p. 242.

5. David Bostock, *The Philosophy of Mathematics: An Introduction* (Chichester: Wiley-Blackwell, 2009), p. 8.

6. Kraut, p. 8.

7. Edith Hamilton and Huntington Cairns, eds., *The Collected Dialogues of Plato* (Princeton: Princeton University Press, 1973), p. 427.

8. David C. Lindberg, *The Beginnings of Western Science* (Chicago: University of Chicago Press, 2007), p. 36.

9. G. E. R. Lloyd, *Early Greek Science: Thales to Aristotle* (New York: W.W. Norton and Co., 1970), pp. 68–69.

10. Cornford, pp. 227–228.

11. Ibid., p. 229.

12. Ibid.

13. Ibid.

14. Ibid., pp. 229–230.

15. Ibid., p. 231.

16. Lindberg, p. 37.

17. Lloyd, p. 79.

Chapter 6. Cosmology

1. Edith Hamilton and Huntington Cairns, eds., *The Collected Dialogues of Plato* (Princeton: Princeton University Press, 1973), p. 1161.

2. G. E. R. Lloyd, *Early Greek Science: Thales to Aristotle* (New York: W.W. Norton and Co., 1970), p. 72.

3. Hamilton and Cairns, p. 1192.

4. David C. Lindberg, *The Beginnings of Western Science* (Chicago: University of Chicago Press, 2007), p. 39.

5. Hamilton and Cairns, pp. 1161–1162.

6. T. K. Johansen, *Plato's Natural Philosophy: A Study of the Timaeus-Critias* (Cambridge: Cambridge University Press, 2004), p. 16.

7. Ibid.

8. Gail Fine, ed., *The Oxford Handbook of Plato* (New York: Oxford University Press, 2008), p. 180.

9. Hamilton and Cairns, pp. 1167–1168.

10. Ibid., p. 1168.

11. Lindberg, p. 41.

12. Hamilton and Cairns, pp 1159–1160.

13. Ibid., pp. 1218–1224.

14. Ibid., p. 1164.

15. Lindberg, p. 40.

16. Ibid.

17. Lloyd, p. 74.

18. Ibid., pp. 76–77.

Chapter 7. Legacy

1. *Dictionary of Scientific Biography*, s.v. "Plato."

2. John Boardman, Jasper green, Oswyn Murray, eds. *The Oxford History of the Classical World* (Oxford: Oxford University Press, 1986), p. 239.

3. Alfred North Whitehead, *Process and Reality*, 1929, quoted in "Plato (428?–348? B.C.)," *International World History Project*, March 16, 2007, <http://history-world.org/plato.htm> (November 19, 2009).

4. G. E. R. Lloyd, *Early Greek Science: Thales to Aristotle* (New York: W.W. Norton and Co., 1970), p. 79.

GLOSSARY

abstract—Considered apart from concrete existence or material objects.

academy—An institution of higher learning or a society for the advancement of art or science.

Academy—The school founded by Plato around 380 B.C. in an area of Athens associated with the hero Academos.

acropolis—A hill or high ground at the heart of a Greek city.

Acropolis—The Acropolis of Athens was a sanctuary to the goddess Athena and home to temples, including the Parthenon.

agora—Marketplace and community center in ancient Greek cities.

allegory—A short story in which people, things, and actions represent an idea about life.

arete—Greek word meaning "virtue" or "excellence."

aristocrats—Members of wealthy landowning families who belonged to the nobility.

circumference—The distance around a circle.

cosmos—The universe; one meaning of the Greek word *kosmos* was "orderly arrangement."

cosmology—The study of the origin and structure of the universe.

decree—An official government order or law.

Demiurge—The divine craftsman Plato credits with creating the cosmos with order and reason.

dialectic—A system of reasoning through an exchange of logical arguments.

element—A basic unit of matter; the Greeks thought that four primary substances—earth, air, fire, and water—were the materials from which all other matter is constructed. In chemistry, elements are any of the more than one hundred known substances that cannot be separated into simpler substances and that either singly or in combination constitute all matter.

empirical—Based on observation and experiment.

ethics—The study of moral values; the study of right and wrong behavior.

Form—Plato's Forms are abstract objects that underlie reality.

frieze—A carved band around the top of a classical building.

gymnasium—A center for exercise and socializing for men in ancient Greece.

hoplite—A Greek soldier; Hoplites wore armor and marched into battle shoulder to shoulder, armed with spears and short swords.

hypotenuse—The longest side of a right triangle.

isosceles triangle—A triangle in which two of the three sides are of equal length.

lyre—A stringed instrument, like a harp, used by ancient Greeks.

paidagogos—A slave who accompanied a Greek boy to school.

philosophy—Rational investigation of questions about existence, knowledge, and ethics.

Platonic solids—Five convex regular polyhedra: the tetrahedron, cube, octahedron, icosahedron, and dodecahedron.

polis—A self-governing Greek city-state.

rhetoric—The art of using language to persuade.

shuttle—A tool used by weavers to guide a thread while making cloth.

stoa—A long Greek building with a columned porch.

theorem—In mathematics, a statement proved on the basis of previously accepted statements.

FURTHER READING

Dell, Pamela. *Socrates : Ancient Greek in Search of Truth*. Minneapolis, Minn.: Compass Point Books, 2007.

Ganeri, Anita. *Ancient Greeks*. Minneapolis, Minn.: Compass Point Books, 2006.

Gow, Mary. *The Great Thinker: Aristotle and the Foundations of Science*. Berkeley Heights, N.J.: Enslow Publishers, Inc., 2011.

McNeely, Ian F., and Wolverton, Lisa. *Reinventing Knowledge: From Alexandria to the Internet*. New York: W. W. Norton, 2008.

Price, Joan. *Ancient and Hellenistic Thought*. New York: Chelsea House, 2007.

Sniderman, Alex. *Plato: The Father of Logic*. New York: Rosen Pub. Group, 2006.

Whiting, Jim. *The Life and Times of Plato*. Hockessin, Del.: Mitchell Lane Publishers, 2007.

INTERNET ADDRESSES

"Plato," University of St. Andrews
http://www-history.mcs.st-and.ac.uk/Mathematicians/
    Plato.html

"Plato" Stanford Encyclopedia of Philosophy
http://plato.stanford.edu/entries/plato/

"Works by Plato," The Internet Classics Archive
http://classics.mit.edu/Browse/browse-Plato.html

INDEX

geometry, 59–60
Glaucon, 23, 64
Gorgias, 38, 66
Greece
    education in, 36–37,
        54–55
    festivals, 29–30
    literacy in, 62
    science in, 15–20
    slavery, 34
    social structure,
        25–26, 31–35
    temples, 27, 28
    women's roles, 33–34
gymnasiums, 54–55

I
icosahedron, 92–96
Iliad (Homer), 24, 62

J
Jupiter, 88, 96, 110

K
Kepler, Johannes, 96–97
knowledge, Plato on, 13

L
Laches, the, 66, 109

M
Mars, 88, 110
mathematics. *see also*
    theory of forms (eidos).
        development of, 58,
            99
        in Greek education,
            37, 57

modern applications
    of, 14–15, 80–81,
    96–98, 105
in Plato's cosmology,
    82–83, 101
Plato's interest in, 10,
    58–59
Republic on, 58
in theory of forms
    (eidos), 70–72, 85
Megara, 25, 51
Menexenus, the, 62
Mercury, 86, 88, 110
metrologia (ratios), 58
momentum, 80
Muses, 55
musical harmonies, 52–53

N
natural world, Plato's
    conception of, 13–14,
    82–89
Newton, Isaac, 97–98

O
observation method,
    60–61, 68–70, 79,
    109–111
octahedron, 92–96
Odyssey (Homer), 24, 62
Olympic Games, 24

P
paidagogos, 24
Panathenaic procession,
    29–30
papyrus, 63
Parthenon, 28, 30, 92